ODD ADAPTATIONS

WHY DO MUDSKIPPERS WALK?

AND OTHER CURIOUS FISH ADAPTATIONS

BY PATRICIA FLETCHER

Gareth Stevens
PUBLISHING

Please visit our website, www.garethstevens.com. For a free color catalog of all our high-quality books, call toll free 1-800-542-2595 or fax 1-877-542-2596.

Cataloging-in-Publication Data

Names: Fletcher, Patricia.
Title: Why do mudskippers walk? And other curious fish adaptations / Patricia Fletcher.
Description: New York : Gareth Stevens Publishing, 2018. | Series: Odd adaptations | Includes index.
Identifiers: ISBN 9781538203934 (pbk.) | ISBN 9781538203958 (library bound) | ISBN 9781538203941 (6 pack)
Subjects: LCSH: Fishes–Adaptation–Juvenile literature. | Adaptation (Biology)–Juvenile literature.
Classification: LCC QL617.2 F54 2018 | DDC 597.14–dc23

First Edition

Published in 2018 by
Gareth Stevens Publishing
111 East 14th Street, Suite 349
New York, NY 10003

Copyright © 2018 Gareth Stevens Publishing

Designer: Sarah Liddell
Editor: Kristen Nelson

Photo credits: Cover, pp. 1, 11 twospeeds/Shutterstock.com; background used throughout Captblack76/
Shutterstock.com; p. 4 StudioSmart/Shutterstock.com; p. 5 (lamprey) Andrei Nekrassov/Shutterstock.com;
p. 5 (tuna) holbox/Shutterstock.com; pp. 6–7 (shark) LeonP/Shutterstock.com; pp. 7, 14 Rich Carey/Shutterstock.com;
p. 8 Alexander Raths/Shutterstock.com; p. 9 Sekar B/Shutterstock.com; p. 10 grafxart/Shutterstock.com;
p. 12 Johannes Komelius/Shutterstock.com; p. 13 Istvan Kovacs/Shutterstock.com; p. 15 Willyam Bradberry/
Shutterstock.com; p. 16 Diriye Amey/Shutterstock.com; p. 17 Brandy McKnight/Shutterstock.com;
p. 18 (top) Konjushenko Vladimir/Shutterstock.com; p. 18 (bottom) Emi/Shutterstock.com; p. 19 Off Axis Production/
Shutterstock.com; p. 21 Norbert Wu/Minden Pictures/Getty Images; p. 22 Mirko Rosenau/Shutterstock.com;
p. 23 Georgette Douwma/Nature Picture Library/Getty Images; p. 24 Drow male/Wikimedia Commons;
p. 25 (stingray) Nantawat Chotsuwan/Shutterstock.com; p. 25 (salmon) IrinaK/Shutterstock.com;
p. 25 (nurse shark) Michael Bogner/Shutterstock.com; p. 25 (largemouth bass) StevenRussellSmithPhotos/
Shutterstock.com; p. 25 (koi) Khumthong/Shutterstock.com; p. 25 (goldfish) Vangert/Shutterstock.com;
p. 26 Beth Swanson/Shutterstock.com; p. 27 Song Heming/Shutterstock.com; p. 28 Bigone/Shutterstock.com;
p. 29 (electric ray) Laura Dinraths/Shutterstock.com; p. 29 (elephantnosed fish) boban_nz/Shutterstock.com;
p. 29 (knifefish) Wildfeuer/Wikimedia Commons.

Printed in China

CONTENTS

Words in the glossary appear in **bold** type the first time they are used in the text.

THE FANTASTIC WORLD OF FISH

What do you picture when you think of a fish? You might think of your goldfish swimming around your fish tank. Or maybe you think of a sunfish you caught when fishing in a lake. There are thousands more species, or kinds, of fish. Some of them look nothing like your goldfish!

Fish are animals that live in water, breathe with gills, and have backbones. **FISH CAN BE SPLIT INTO GROUPS THAT ARE VERY DIFFERENT FROM ONE ANOTHER BECAUSE OF THE MANY ADAPTATIONS EACH GROUP HAS DEVELOPED.** Though important to the fish's survival, these adaptations can seem incredibly odd to us!

MANTA RAY

KINDS OF FISH

CLASS/ COMMON NAME	COMMON FEATURES	EXAMPLES
AGNATHA/ JAWLESS FISH	LACK A JAW; NO SCALES	LAMPREYS, HAGFISH
CHONDRICHTHYES/ CARTILAGINOUS FISH	SKELETON MADE OF **CARTILAGE**	SHARKS, RAYS
OSTEICHTHYES/ BONY FISH	JAW PRESENT; SKELETON MADE OF BONES	TUNA, BASS, SALMON

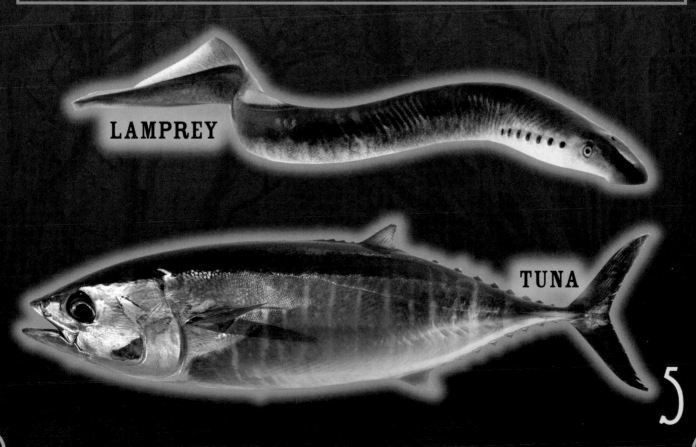

LAMPREY

TUNA

ALL OVER EARTH

There are fish living in almost every natural body of water on Earth. Fish are found in so many different places because they've adapted as Earth changed over time. **MODERN FISH ARE THE RESULT OF MILLIONS OF YEARS OF EVOLUTION!**

Fish **habitats** range from shallow freshwater ponds where koi live, to estuaries where you might find salmon and mackerel, to the open ocean where sharks can be found. There are even fish that live tens of thousands of feet below the surface!

SHARK

UNDER PRESSURE

Fish all share one cool adaptation: the ability to sense changes in water pressure and water currents. Their bodies have small canals in their skin, commonly around the eyes and mouth and down the side of the body, that help them know about changes in the water **environment** around them.

SOME FISH, LIKE THE MACKEREL SHOWN HERE, HAVE ADAPTED TO LIVING IN ESTUARIES, OR PLACES WHERE FRESHWATER AND SALT WATER MEET.

DON'T GET SALTY

Fish need water and a certain amount of salt in their body to live. Depending on whether a fish lives in freshwater or salt water, it will have adaptations to keep this balance just right.

FRESHWATER FISH BARELY DRINK WATER! They take in enough of it through their skin. In order to have the right amount of salt, though, they have special cells in their gills and mouths that collect extra salt from the water.

SALTWATER FISH DRINK LOTS OF WATER, BUT DON'T EXCRETE MOST OF IT. They do have to get rid of some salt they take in through their waste.

SALMON

PART-TIME HOME

Some fish can live in both salt water and freshwater! These are called euryhaline fish, and they can withstand a range of salinity, or saltiness, in water. This ability to adapt to different salinity is uncommon, partly because in order to adapt to changes in salinity, a fish's body has to use a lot of energy.

SALMON SPEND MOST OF THEIR LIFE IN THE OCEAN, BUT THEY TRAVEL UP FRESHWATER RIVERS AND STREAMS TO **SPAWN**. SALMON BABIES MAY LEAVE THE FRESHWATER RIGHT AFTER BIRTH OR STAY UP TO 2 YEARS!

9

Fish are a varied animal group! The largest fish on Earth, the whale shark, can weigh 21 tons (19 mt) and be almost as long as a school bus! The smallest fish, a kind of carp, is only about 0.3 inch (8 mm) long. Fish's size and body shape have developed over time to make them better able to live in their habitat!

Rays and flounders live on the bottom of the ocean. **THEY HAVE VERY FLAT BODIES, PERFECT FOR HIDING AND MOVING AROUND IN THEIR HABITAT.** They move by undulating their fins or body, which means moving in waves!

STINGRAY

10

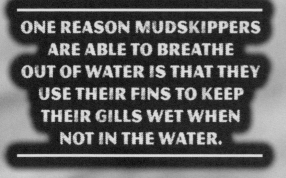

ONE REASON MUDSKIPPERS ARE ABLE TO BREATHE OUT OF WATER IS THAT THEY USE THEIR FINS TO KEEP THEIR GILLS WET WHEN NOT IN THE WATER.

TAKING A WALK

Mudskippers aren't great swimmers. They "walk" on the bottom of the swampy areas where they live. But they can also use their leg-shaped fins to push themselves *out* of the water to "walk" on land to look for food! Climbing perch and some catfishes can also leave the water by wiggling or using fins to "walk" to escape predators.

11

Depending on their class, fish may have scales or even bony plates covering their body. The coloring of these scales or plates can help fish blend in to where they live. The crocodile fish's **camouflage** is even better! IN ORDER TO HIDE FROM THE PREY IT'S WAITING FOR, THE CROCODILE FISH GROWS SKIN OVER ITS DARK EYES THAT LOOKS LIKE LACE—AND THE SANDY AREAS WHERE IT LIVES!

Fish can be many bright colors, too! These colors may let other fish know a fish's territory. Special coloring might also be so a species of fish can recognize others like it.

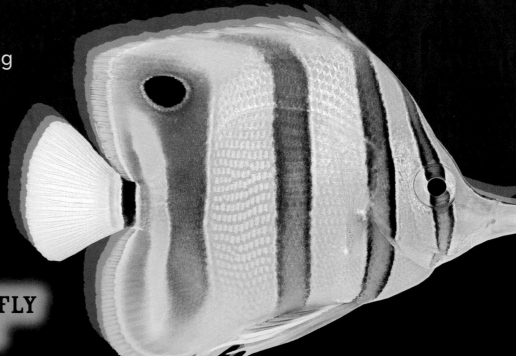

BUTTERFLY FISH

12

CROCODILE FISH ARE ALSO KNOWN AS DE BEAUFORT'S FLATHEADS OR GIANT FLATHEADS. THEY LIVE—AND HIDE—IN **REEFS**.

13

CHOWING DOWN

Many fish eat other fish and **invertebrates**. They've adapted to have exactly the kind of mouth and teeth they need!

Parrot fish have a pointed mouth somewhat like a bird's beak. Their teeth are short and strong in order to break off pieces of coral to get at the **algae** growing on it. **PARROT FISH, LIKE MANY OTHER FISH, ALSO HAVE THROAT TEETH!** This adaptation sounds scary, but it's important. Throat teeth help parrot fish crush coral pieces. They help other fish move their food into the tube that leads to their stomach, the esophagus.

PARROT FISH

RAKE IT IN!

Some fish that eat **plankton** have many tiny rods made of bone or cartilage on their gills. These gill rakers make sure the tiny planktons in a fish's mouth can't escape through the gill openings. Then, the planktons are moved to the fish's throat to be swallowed.

DESPITE HAVING TEETH, MOST FISH SWALLOW THEIR PREY WHOLE. GREAT WHITE SHARKS LIKE THIS ONE USE THEIR TEETH TO RIP PREY INTO SMALLER PIECES AND SWALLOW THOSE WHOLE.

FISH SENSE

Fish may have incredible senses of smell, taste, and sight—but not all fish need all three senses to be great. **SOME EELS HAVE VERY SMALL EYES AND HAVE DEVELOPED A GREAT SENSE OF SMELL IN ORDER TO FIND FOOD.**

Many fish have taste buds! Some can taste with other parts of their body, too. **CATFISH, WHICH DON'T SEE WELL, HAVE EXTRA BODY PARTS FOR TASTING CALLED BARBELS.** They look like whiskers and earned catfish their name!

Many fish must hear well, too. Because sound travels quickly underwater, fish can use sounds to talk to each other. Damselfish make noise when trying to protect their territory!

FISH TALK

Fish communicate with sounds made many ways, including using their throat teeth or swim bladders, a body part that helps them stay afloat. Most sounds have to do with a fish in trouble or mating. The fish in one group are called drums or croakers because they're known to make lots of noise at spawning time!

EEL

16

CATFISH USE THEIR BARBELS TO SEARCH FOR FOOD ON THE BOTTOM OF THE FRESHWATER HABITATS THEY LIVE IN AROUND THE WORLD.

There's more to a fish's sense of smell than just food! **FISH GIVE OFF CHEMICALS TO COMMUNICATE DIFFERENT INFORMATION TO OTHER FISH AROUND THEM.**

When injured, a minnow gives off a chemical to let other minnows know there is danger.

Some baby fish give off a chemical that tells their parents to stay close—and not to eat them!

Young fish can often find other fish of their kind by the chemicals they give off.

Female fish also put certain chemicals in the water to let male fish know they're ready to mate and lay eggs.

WHAT CHEMICALS?

The chemicals fish—and other animals—give off to talk to each other are called pheromones. To other animals, these chemical messages might seem like a regular smell. But to the animals receiving the message, they mean so much more! These smells aren't commonly made on purpose, either. They're just natural parts of animal, and fish, communication.

MINNOWS

YOU CAN'T SEE IT, BUT THIS SCHOOL OF MINNOWS MIGHT BE COMMUNICATING RIGHT NOW!

19

LET THERE BE LIGHT

Deep-sea fish have adaptations to make up for the darkness of their habitat, which can be thousands of feet below the surface. **THE LANTERN FISH HAS A HEADLIGHT!** It's a body part on their nose that lights up. Lantern fish also have other light-producing body parts called photophores on their underside.

The black dragonfish has photophores on its body, too. When it's bothered, it can light up all over its body—even all along its fins! Most living things that light up give off a blue-green light.

BLACK DRAGONFISH CAN GLOW A RED COLOR THAT'S ALMOST INFRARED! Some animals, including people, can't see infrared light. It keeps the black dragonfish from being seen as it hunts!

BIOLUMINESCENCE

When a living thing gives off light, it's called bioluminescence. Some animals are bioluminescent because of body parts like photophores, but others light up because they eat a certain kind of bacteria! Fish use bioluminescence to see better in dark water, draw in prey, or find a mate.

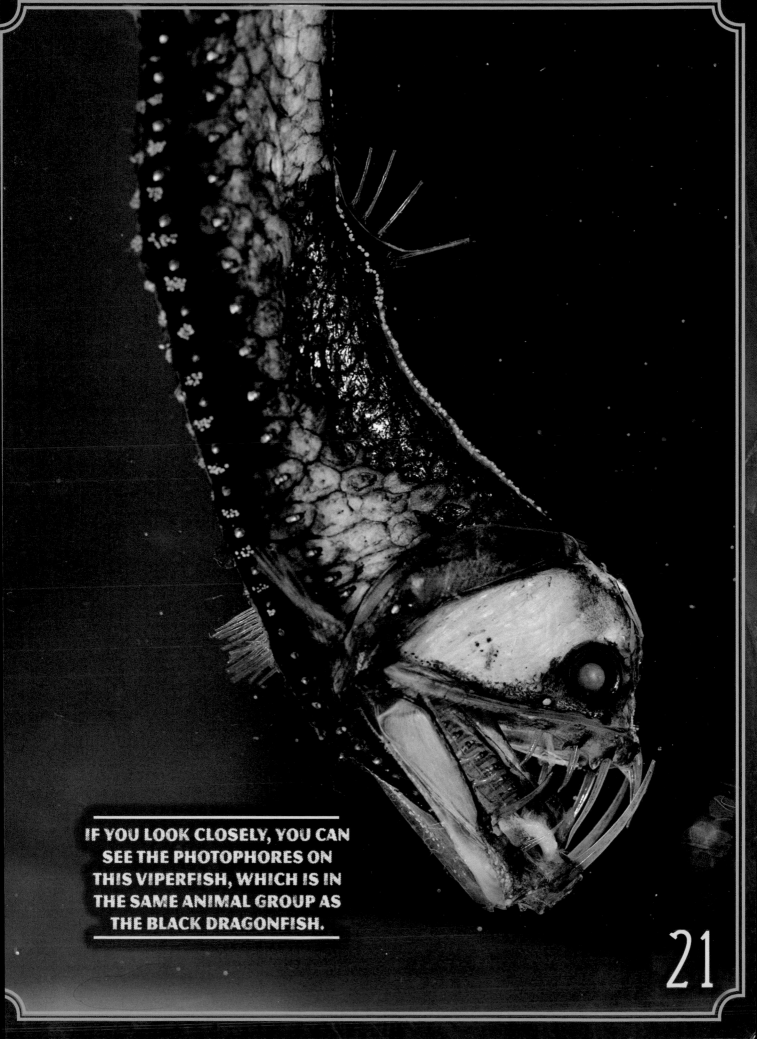

IF YOU LOOK CLOSELY, YOU CAN
SEE THE PHOTOPHORES ON
THIS VIPERFISH, WHICH IS IN
THE SAME ANIMAL GROUP AS
THE BLACK DRAGONFISH.

21

LIVING THE FISH LIFE

Most fish have a similar life cycle, but adaptations within it have developed over time so each species has a good chance at survival. Most fish lay eggs, but how long it takes for them to hatch depends on the fish. It can take a few days or a few weeks.

Jawfish are one kind of mouth-brooding fish. **ONCE A FEMALE JAWFISH LAYS EGGS, THE MALE JAWFISH HOLDS THEM IN HIS MOUTH UNTIL THEY HATCH!** The eggs are held together by sticky matter called mucus. The only time the male jawfish sets the eggs down is when he eats.

GOURAMI

NESTING

Fish sometimes make nests to keep their eggs safe! Sticklebacks build nests made of plants and sticky matter they excrete. **GOURAMIS BLOW BUBBLES MADE OF MUCUS AND LAY EGGS INSIDE THEM!** Other fish have simpler nesting behaviors, such as making a small hole in the sand or mud at the bottom of a body of water.

"BROOD" MEANS TO CARE FOR EGGS IN ORDER TO GET THEM TO HATCH. THAT'S WHY JAWFISH LIKE THIS ONE ARE CALLED MOUTH-BROODERS.

23

Most fish stay larvae for only a few weeks. Not lampreys! **LAMPREYS STAY LARVAE FOR 5 YEARS OR MORE.** These larvae burrow into the sand or dirt of the freshwater streams or rivers where they were born, leaving only their mouthlike oral hood out. As water passes over them, the larvae filter out, or strain, their food.

Some kinds of sharks give birth to live young. Others lay eggs that hatch later! The spiny dogfish shark probably has the longest gestation period, or time of carrying a baby, of any animal with a backbone. **SPINY DOGFISH MOTHERS CARRY BABIES INSIDE THEIR BODY FOR ALMOST 2 YEARS!**

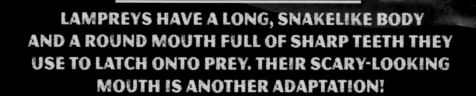

LAMPREYS HAVE A LONG, SNAKELIKE BODY AND A ROUND MOUTH FULL OF SHARP TEETH THEY USE TO LATCH ONTO PREY. THEIR SCARY-LOOKING MOUTH IS ANOTHER ADAPTATION!

AVERAGE FISH LIFE-SPANS

SOCKEYE SALMON
16 YEARS

STINGRAY
15 TO 20 YEARS

LARGEMOUTH BASS
16 YEARS

NURSE SHARK
25 YEARS

LIFE-SPAN

The life-span of different fish can vary. Small fish may only live 1 to 3 years. Some kinds of fish can live to be 100. Greenland sharks have been found to live even longer than that! SCIENTISTS STUDIED ONE GREENLAND SHARK THEY BELIEVE LIVED ABOUT 400 YEARS.

KOI
25 TO 35 YEARS

GOLDFISH
30 YEARS

PROTECT AND DEFEND

Adaptations often develop for animals' protection. The stonefish has two major adaptations to stay safe. The first is great camouflage. It looks just like the rocks and coral it lives among! It's also one of the most poisonous fish in the world. **STONEFISH HAVE 13 SHARP SPINES FULL OF STRONG VENOM THAT CAUSE PAINFUL STINGS!**

Pufferfish have had to develop protection, too. They aren't very good swimmers! When scared, a pufferfish will take in a lot of water and puff out their stomach to look bigger. **IF A PREDATOR DOES TAKE A BITE, PUFFERFISH CONTAIN A TOXIN THAT WILL KILL IT!**

PUFFERFISH TOXINS ARE DEADLY TO PEOPLE, TOO. NONETHELESS, SOME PEOPLE EAT PUFFERFISH! SPECIAL CHEFS HAVE LEARNED HOW TO PREPARE IT TO AVOID SERVING THE POISONOUS PARTS.

SAFETY IN NUMBERS

Many kinds of fish move together in order to better keep away from predators. Sardines travel in big groups called schools partly for this reason. However, over time their feeding and mating behavior adapted to schooling, too!

27

Some kinds of fish have a shocking adaptation they use for hunting prey. **ELECTRIC EELS CAN MAKE THEIR OWN ELECTRIC FIELDS!** The strength of the electric field depends on the size of the eel, but some can stun their prey with it! Electric rays can also stun prey with electric fields. Other fish, such as skates and other rays, can make weaker electric fields, but only use them to find food, mates, or travel around underwater.

There are so many odd adaptations in the fish world! Scientists are discovering more all the time. What crazy colors or awesome anatomy will they find next?

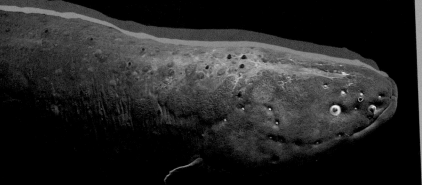

ELECTRIC EEL

JUST KEEP ADAPTING

Fish have been evolving and adapting for hundreds of millions of years. So far, they've been able to find ways to survive in the ever-changing water habitats of Earth. If we take care of Earth and its valuable water, there's no reason to believe fish won't continue to evolve long into the future!

ELECTRIC
RAY

ALL THESE FISH USE A SPECIAL
BODY PART TO PRODUCE
ELECTRIC FIELDS.

KNIFEFISH

ELEPHANTNOSE
FISH

GLOSSARY

algae: plantlike living things that are mostly found in water

blood vessel: a small tube in an animal's body that carries blood

camouflage: colors or shapes in animals that allow them to blend in with their surroundings

cartilage: tough, bendable tissue that makes up part or all of a skeleton

develop: to grow and change

environment: the conditions that surround a living thing and affect the way it lives

evolution: the process of animals and plants slowly changing into new forms over thousands of years

excrete: to give off, commonly waste

habitat: the natural place where an animal or plant lives

invertebrate: an animal without a backbone

plankton: a tiny plant or animal that floats in the ocean

reef: a chain of rocks or coral, or a ridge of sand, at or near the water's surface

spawn: a way some marine animals reproduce in which eggs are let loose in the water

FOR MORE INFORMATION

BOOKS

Midthun, Joseph, and Samuel Hiti. *Plant and Animal Adaptations.* Chicago, IL: World Book, 2014.

Niver, Heather Moore. *Marine Fossils.* New York, NY: PowerKids Press, 2017.

Pettiford, Rebecca. *Puffer Fish.* Minneapolis, MN: Bellwether Media, Inc., 2017.

WEBSITES

Fish
kids.nationalgeographic.com/animals/hubs/fish/
Learn about and see pictures of many kinds of fish.

Fish
www.ducksters.com/animals/fish.php
Read even more about fish on this website for kids!

Mudskippers: Walking Fish
channel.nationalgeographic.com/videos/mudskippers-walking-fish/
Watch a video of mudskippers walking out of the water!

INDEX